The Rest of the World

Also by Norman Jope

For the Wedding-Guest (Stride, 1996)
The Book of Bells and Candles (Waterloo Press, 2009)
Dreams of the Caucasus (Shearsman Books, 2010)
Aphinar (Waterloo Press, 2012)
Gólyák és Rétesek (trans. Zoltán Tarcsay: FISZ-Apokrif, 2018)
Portland: a Triptych (with Tim Allen and Mark Goodwin; KFS, 2019)

The Rest
of the World

Norman Jope

Shearsman Books

First published in the United Kingdom in 2021 by
Shearsman Books Ltd
PO Box 4239
Swindon
SN3 9FN

Shearsman Books Ltd Registered Office
30–31 St. James Place, Mangotsfield, Bristol BS16 9JB
(this address not for correspondence)

www.shearsman.com

ISBN 978-1-84861-789-6

Copyright © Norman Jope, 2021.

The right of Norman Jope to be identified as the author of this work
has been asserted by him in accordance with the
Copyrights, Designs and Patents Act of 1988.
All rights reserved.

Cover illustration copyright ©Lynda Stevens, 2021.

Acknowledgements

Some of these works, or earlier versions of them, have appeared in *A Festschrift for Tony Frazer*, *Epizootics!*, *Litter*, *Shearsman* and *Stride*. Hungarian translations of some of these works have appeared in *Apokrif*, *Gólyák és Rétesek* and *2000*.

CONTENTS

I. VIRTUAL VOYAGES

Geo-Delirium	11
Nordkapp	12
Seals in Stromness	13
In Corleone	14
On a Road Near Mezőtúr	15
Moldova	16
Addis Ababa	17
Mombasa	18
Waiting for a Guide in Clarksdale	19
A Topographical Misunderstanding	20
10th November 1891	21

II. POINTS OF ENTRY · 25

III. A LIFE WITHIN A LIFE

A Reconstruction	33
Comrade Rain	34
In Óbuda's Bricolage	35
The Red Steering Wheel	36
Almost out of Breath	37
A Heron's Adventure	38
An Incremental Voyage	39
Coda	40
Old Stones, White Roads	41
Kazimierz	42
The Rest of the World	43

IV. ON A DRY SEA · 47

V. DESIRE AND HARM

    Flesh Horizon   57
    By Brazilian Waters   58
    Sightings of the Mystery Woman   59
    Lightness of Touch   60
    Out of Focus   61
    A Heckler in El Club Silencio   62
    The Gatecrashers   63
    Three Denouements (after Herzog)   64
    Kaspar and the Volumes   65
    Bariloche   66
    Tangerine Dream in the Third Reich   67

VI. A CITIZEN'S DIARY   71

VII. RENDITIONS OF HOME

    Climbing the Sky   81
    Ubiquity   82
    Collecting the Past in My Hands   83
    When Every Song Was New   84
    A Promenade in Dunsburgh   85
    Girders Between the Stars   86
    The Hidden Land Hides Me   87
    Keeping Vigil   88
    Out of My Hands   89
    Altogether Elsewhere   90
    Unseen   91

*For Lynda, my partner in a thirty-five-year flight,
and for a soft landing to come.*

Virtual voyages

GEO-DELIRIUM

Succumbing to the temptations of Google Earth, I travel manically from place to place whilst, to my right, the view from the window remains unchanged apart from the flight of a chaffinch and the trembling of a bush.

From Prague to Patmos, from Plympton South Australia to its originating namesake, all journeys are equal. The cyber-plane takes off and, after moments of blur, one lands in the place that one has named as if for the very first time.

'All this shall be yours' he said 'if you will bow down and worship me'. Greedy for the spaces of earth, I land in the rocky brilliance of Patmos and enter the Cave of the Apocalypse. There's a white wall with a recess for the saint's head… outside, the burning slopes that are still set in a sapphire sea on a February night, as if the seasons had become an irrelevance.

From Patmos I return to Dunwich via Sighisoara – a journey that would take a number of days, traversed in moments. I arrive – first scrambled then unscrambled – in a back street of stucco-fronted houses. The Transylvanian countryside can be glimpsed to the right. It is as quiet as when I walked that street over six years ago, but my absence taunts me as I move my mouse in the direction of the Saxon graveyard.

In Dunwich, I look for Sebald in the only street – a street surprisingly devoid of historical atmosphere, neat like a cul-de-sac in a suburb. Driving, or walking, or perhaps flying to the beach I find myself circling, panning the view and aware that, with a few strokes of the keyboard, I can return home… if such a concept still holds meaning.

NORDKAPP

Driving north on the E69 in a vehicle of air, I see that it is April. Despite this, snow covers most of the ground and what is uncovered is a ruddy brown tundra. On either side, there are views of distant cliffs and the Barents Sea deflects equinoctial light. The sky is almost metallic in its pale blues and pinks.

There is not a trace of life in sight, no hare, no ptarmigan, no midge. I pass through the checkpoint, beyond the superfluous speed sign that fixes my velocity, by law, at seventy kilometres an hour – but the speed of the connection holds me back and, as I advance, the landscape blurs into jagged pastel shards and Turneresque washes.

Beyond the checkpoint whose red and white barrier is as incongruous here as an orange grove, playing Terje Rypdal's 'Rolling Stone' through my headphones, I register the cold with my eyes but not my skin. Impasto icings layer the landscape and wheel-tracks pierce them like *sastrugi* – up ahead, the Vilfred Pettersen hut is a flattened pagoda and the raised sphere of the Nordkapphallen is the captured moon of another planet.

Here the road ends, even though the music persists and Svein Christiansen's delicate drumming, all cymbals and syncopation, under- and over-scores Rypdal's guitar as the obelisk shines mutely and, at the entrance to the hall, the exact latitude of 71 degrees 10 minutes 21 seconds north is displayed in white on yellow.

I stand there for a moment, lost in contemplation of the uncountable miles behind me. I register the cold with my mind and not my skin, but it still exhilarates with its chill.

SEALS IN STROMNESS

for Roderick Muncey

In a smashed-up whaling station recessed into the corner of a city gallery, we watch sleet fall as we feel it with our minds. That is cold enough on a mild day in British winter, when traffic merges with the grunting of fur seals that have taken over the dismantled fittings and rotting furniture. They forage pointlessly across the shambled floor, or lie in shadows gaping like dossers. They arrange themselves in formation on the beach, beside a crumbling pier, watching grey surf as sleet's blown in. They lollop like Malone and the Unnameable. They move their bulk like cattle crossing a farmyard on the *puszta*. They investigate the wreckage like the Stalker and his companions. The world has ended and the aftermath is ruination, sleet on bare hillsides, an indifferent tribe of reindeer moving their sinews at the holocaust's verge.

We watch sleet fall, we stay for a second and third screening… amused and dazzled by the repetition. It is during the third screening that the the writer-in-residence appears with her retinue of short-term courtiers. She offers us a paragraph of her own interpretation but, no matter how eloquent her words, they are as nothing to the silence of the camera, the stillness of images that embody our extinction.

As if baffled by our indifference to her words, she withdraws her crocodile of eager families with the tart riposte – 'let's leave those guys to their fur seals'. But the seals were only the psychopomps. *There are still songs to be sung*, as has again been proved, *on the other side of humankind*.

This piece is based on a video by Simon Faithfull, shown at the Peninsula Art Gallery, Plymouth as part of the 'Landscapes of Exploration' exhibition (January – March 2012). This Stromness is located in South Georgia, not the Orkneys.

IN CORLEONE

Outside the Central Bar, a young man in a ski jacket keeps watch – there's something tucked under his arm but it's impossible to tell what it is. Beside him, a painting of three rustics adorns the bar. Each has something sharp in their hand but it's impossible to tell what from this angle. On the other side of the door, there's a poster advertising Il Padrino – a herbal liqueur in a long slim violet bottle. It's almost impossible to see inside and impossible to step through that door from here. Only a man in a bottle-green coat and navy jeans, half-obscured, his back to the camera, evades my curiosity.

Everywhere, as expected, the plasterwork is peeled and venerable and there's a worn-down balcony on every facade. There are very few people about at this time of the morning in the evening, as I glide from street to street on a milk-white vector. Up the Via Roma and back down again, to the Via Bentivegna, taking in the electric air, watching for signs of intrigue I am invisible – unlike the vehicle from which this footage was taken – scanning faces that have been thoughtfully blurred so that even the girls, on the poster outside the Solo Gioielli boutique, are as inscrutable as sphinxes.

In this day without a date, at this time without a time, I am unwelcome but nobody knows it – this is not a place, I think, that would betray its secrets without a price. I recall the hilltop towns I know and compare Corleone to Shaftesbury and Launceston, imagining the murderous mobs that they might have secreted under conditions of heat and poverty.

At an elevation of 558 metres above sea level, passing a stray brown dog, I exit by way of the Via Spatafora but the road is blocked by the disappearance of my possible route. Perhaps – given all I've seen – it's as well that I'm able to emerge unscathed with a single click of the mouse.

ON A ROAD NEAR MEZŐTÚR

The rutted road is reaching into the *puszta* on a January day. There are so many puddles that it would be possible to leap from one to the next, all the way down, without touching dry land. On either side of the rutted road, anorexic aspens are fixed in a wind that is also fixed – in this permanent moment, it is completely without force.

On either side of the road, there are also *tanyák* – isolated farmsteads – visible across wide, ploughed empty fields that the snow has either left or has not yet fallen on. It's mild for January and the *puszta* is brown, not white. There's nothing to be seen, neither beast nor bird, and the silence is absolute – only yellow post boxes break the monotony, and fly-tipped garbage like entropic flowers.

At the far end of the road, the footage gives out and a muddy track continues to who knows where. For this is where the eyes turn back. They swivel full circle, taking in the emptiness and muteness on every side. They are as homeless as probes from another galaxy – landing on earth at random, drinking in what little evidence there is at the end of a long and rutted road.

That muddy track might lead, across the Carpathians and the Ukrainian steppe, into the very centre of Asia. And that baleful sky will certainly lead to constellations that hide from sight – as if everywhere were near and simultaneously thwarted. This still life comes to life once more as I watch it, turning one more circle before heading back to my desk.

MOLDOVA

Fate propels me there, with my tiny pension and my neighbours plotting as I sit on the veranda of my cottage, in a village three hours' grimy-windowed bus-ride from the capital, and drain draught after draught of cheap wine like the doctor draining apricot brandy in *Sátántangó*. I will enter my eighth decade learning a new language with headstrong incompetence, a Rich Man from the West who is not rich at all and does not understand anything, who is swindled with justification by handymen with large families to feed, who is propositioned by women a third of his age although his erections, these days, are almost exclusively in the mind. I will be the perfect subject for a film that is never made as my friends send e-mails from the depths of Devon and the backwoods of freezing, pristine Canada, as I skype them on dial-up knocking over everything and staring into the webcam like a Seventies police sergeant giving his suspect the treatment. You, my lover, will be giving English lessons exactly a thousand miles to the east, as now, which probably places you somewhere in Kazakhstan. I will apply the usual forbearance as I learn to draw wood and chop water, then learn to learn from my mistakes – out at sunset, watching the clouds turn dark over vine-and-sunflower covered hills of the Moldovan interior, having no home but the death I still stave off at any cost, enjoying the flora and fauna and reading the books I stacked up in my more prosperous fifties. What innocence fate has in store for me! I think, contemplating this land that is named after a drowned dog in a fable, the poorest in Europe and the only one without a guidebook to its name… its shape the very shape of my fate, its undeserved failures my own, its wine the blood that flows in my veins. I can smell its cigarette smoke as I write and sense its undulations under my feet.

ADDIS ABABA

I am there and not there, walking pocked pavements with the weary and the wary, listening to Mulatu Astatqe's ethno-jazz and thinking back to the florid shirts of the early Seventies. I have no sense of the geography of this city that I wander in, stared at by sad-faced young men in brown jackets and disdained by Abyssinian maids with brightly-coloured headscarves. I have no clear sense of a centre, and Le Corbusier boulevards give way to shacks and corrugated panels.

Signs declaim wares in syncopated English, and the eyes of jackals are upon me as I parch – or so I imagine. Not one of the seven million inhabitants can lead me out of this labyrinth. I reach into my pocket and all that it contains is sand from the Danakil Desert.

Cherkos, Kebena, Urael, Kazanchis… I drift from district to district, dodging vendors whose goods I cannot afford to buy this evening. So can I bluff my way into the Sheraton, 'the best of the best' and revive myself in a marble bath? Or beg and cajole my way to a plate of fasting *wat*? Night will fall soon. I wander up Churchill Avenue, with its most English of names post-liberation, asking myself if it was ever Via Mussolini.

I colonise this city with my *dérive*, like an Emperor who, with a sweep of his hand, claims lands the size of Spain from his raft. The city will be named after me when I am dead (I hallucinate) and the Lion of Judah will roar at my grave-side.

To be there and not there at all, wanting to be there in the land of antelopes, strolling like a ghost as rain begins to fall.

MOMBASA

The first thing one notices are wires, strung across the outside of buildings like spaghetti.

Then shutters, balconies, a man in a basketball shirt pushing a trailer down a street. A child in an orange top, waving at no-one in particular.

In the Old Town, there are even more spectacular balconies. Tattooed with intricate carvings, they are set in dove-white walls. But sweat pours into my eyes. My throat is a chasm of dryness through which I plunge.

Dazed, I pass charcoal sellers and tuk-tuks, my mind besieged by Coca-Cola signs and urgent graffiti. The city is strung together with wires. It fizzes and sparkles with its connectivity.

In the market, black-clad female vendors shelter under enormous parasols. I look up at closed shutters and hallucinate myself inside their shaded rooms, as old as I have ever been and as young as in the days of the Morris Minor.

Shop-signs are painted on white walls – the roughly-drawn barber shears his customer. The weight in my head is thickening. My hair is matted with sweat from my indolent brow.

Inside Fort Jesus, I rest amongst cannons and palms, anonymous behind its ochre walls. Outside, the sea conducts its trade with the wind.

Invisible wires go through my skull and it is as though I will never leave. The messages of this frenetic, faded port will remain mysterious, coming clear only in whispers.

WAITING FOR A GUIDE IN CLARKSDALE

Mercurial roads are steeped in a slippery light. Amongst flat-pak buildings and magnolias I search for the blues… but find Domino's Pizza outlets instead and so many filling stations that it is hard to tell where the cars they service are hidden. In fact, the roads are almost empty. They reflect the light that brands my forehead and my eyes are filled with a water as intense as Bourbon.

On Desoto Avenue, I elude the gazes of the few who are out and about in midday heat. The Desoto Shopping Centre appears to have vanished, but I cannot decipher the signs. A freight train crosses the bridge – the number, ACFX 73142, is no help to me at all. I'm swamped in near-namelessness. There's a Gucci advert on the rail bridge but, every time I strain to look at it, my focus slips to the other side.

I guess it's time to go, I advise myself with antecedents in mind. But the only pact that I have made is with technology.

Highway 61 to the south – New Africa Road – leaves the town behind for a landscape that, in its arable flatness, is more reminiscent of the Hungarian *puszta*, or the Fens, than any photograph of Africa that I have seen. And, crushed by consistent sky, he walks before me. A guitar is slung across his shoulder. A harmonica is tied to his neck.

As with the *puszta*, the spaciousness is exquisitely tortuous in its monotony. Water burns in roadside channels and I cannot catch him up – he walks at a demon's pace and I falter like the impostor I am, longing for shelter and a landscape that curves with the body's undulations.

A TOPOGRAPHICAL MISUNDERSTANDING

for Werner Herzog

Six years after describing the 'Caucasus' of Kaspar Hauser's dream as *'the tidy landscape of a train-set, surveyed on flickering film'*, I discover its origin in a study of your work by Brad Prager, subtitled 'aesthetic ecstasy and truth'.

He quotes you, talking about your brother Lucki Stipetić:

'He was in Burma when he was 19 and with an 8 mm camera he shot this vast plain with hundreds of temples in it... I shot it through a semi-transparent screen from the other side (and) filmed it with 35 mm, all of which gives the image a 'mysterious shutter effect.'[1]

And this is what led to my conception of 'the tidy landscape of a train-set' – conceived in the forty-seven seconds of this sequence, committed rapidly to typescript on a screen and two years later, with significant care, to print.

In penance, I imagine a model railway laid down amongst the *stupas* of Myanmar, with plastic figures of signalmen and stationmasters mingling with Buddhist monks and peasants. Yet my folly only proves your artistry. This footage, taken so far from its origins, became exactly what I, the viewer, wanted it to be. But anything but the Caucasus, still, which was the point of the exercise.

Yet I'm as far removed from the landscapes of Ararat and Erebus as was Kaspar, in the garden, sharing his dream with a sympathetic critic.

---

[1] *Herzog's words are quoted in Brad Prager,* The Cinema of Werner Herzog *(Wallflower, 2007).*

10TH NOVEMBER 1891

He swims from one world to the next. A pain as deep as the sea surrounds him, obsessing him with insatiable colours. Seen through a microscope he secretes in the depths of his mind, the cancer that spread from his limb to the rest of his body reveals itself as a garden of implacable flowers. Once more, he decamps… making space for an innocence that barges him aside.

Delirious, he states his destination and the world, amassed behind him like a squadron of signs, pursues him to the ultimate lighthouse. He feigns conversion, as an act of kindness, to throw his grieving relatives off the scent. For his one true god is adventure, his nemesis boredom. The nocturnal sky, his chosen blanket, offers its southern stars in homage.

His voice resounds to the vagabonds of our own time, to migrants whose knapsacks are splashed with mud – on the move through sunflower fields where newly-erected barbed wire shines. He was the first on the move, it seems, but only because of the words he wrote. They moved more rapidly than any that came before him – and continue to do so.

Points of Entry

Hungary, April 2012

*

The Basilica at Esztergom, the Belváros and the grid-iron streets of Kispest give way to the landing-strip. Again, I tangle my world-line with ten million Hungarians – my shadow, pitched in various directions, will collide with those of natives and exiles. When I leave, the history of my shadows – like that of my footsteps – will be inscribed on pavement and street, an invisible thickness that will nonetheless remain. The ink in my pen approximates that shadow.

*

The following morning, in the Allee Mall in Buda, I watch the shoppers pass and wonder how it would look if only their shadows were visible. Or how it would be if they were the shadows of their shadows.

*

So it is that recognition blurs with discovery. Here in this mall for the first time in two years, I pit my recollections against its reality. What books did I look at in Libri? What drinks did we order and in what café? Following the faded scent of myself, I lay a trail for my successors.

*

The open-air gallery shows photographs of the art of Endre Rozsda – an interleaving of eyes and fronds. What shadows would these images cast, if they were in three dimensions, on the delicate shadows of Várfok Utca?

*

In the Soviet Zen Garden of the Memento Park, haranguers harangue emptiness: busts of bespectacled officials squint at the light: heroes, exiled after death, pursue their ossified struggles. Today, there are only two visitors – we are entering a phase in which the memory of that era has almost gone, and in which the memory of that memory foments an enigma. Perhaps, in another ten years, the site may revert to a pissing-patch for dogs – and the statues, packed neatly into warehouses, will keep the faith amongst themselves.

*

The adversary's eyes are so often indecipherable. This is oddly consoling – surely they cannot share our desires, our flaws, our common humanity.

*

Places one visits infrequently but regularly, like this café in the Várhegy, store up one's shadows so that they rise, in greeting, on one's return. The last time I was here, in August, the table was sticky with my sweat. The time before that was in January, and the heater struggled to ward off the cold. Now, on a mild April morning, equilibrium has been reached in what seems like less than an hour.

*

A stall in the Népliget coach station sells t-shirts and sweatshirts – many are of a nationalist stamp, with the pre-Trianon map of Hungary or the red-and-white stripes of the Árpád flag. The proprietor, who beckons to a potential customer, is Chinese and speaks Hungarian with a slurred, faltering accent.

*

Eighty-five kilometres to the south, László Báron's image of Kecskemét is of a 'város a homokon' – a city built on sand. The street map of the city inspires his abstract painting – different shades of sand are glued to the canvas, full of the *puszta's* scorching heat.

*

This is my fourth visit to the city of goats ('Kecske' is the Hungarian for 'goat', and a leaping *kecske* adorns the city's coat of arms). It feels as though I am walking through myself. Two veggie burgers, eaten almost six years apart on (quite possibly) the same bench from (quite possibly) the same tray… the one I ate an hour ago sustains the ghost of my forty-five-year-old self, whilst I ruminate upon the invisible ghost of its predecessor with my fifty-one-year-old teeth.

*

Dining alone in what I mistook to be the restaurant of the Hotel Aranyhomok (the 'hotel of the golden sands') – it turns out to be the lobby bar – The Eagles' 'Hotel California' accompanies me as I eat outnumbered by staff. I'm in a so-called 'Wellness' hotel and, through a plate glass window, there are white dressing gowns and overweight bodies splashing about. They also dance to the tune of Hotel California, as if none of us were able to leave our separate fish-tanks.

*

On this Holy Thursday, a procession in white raiment crosses the main square and enters the Great Church to the sound of bells that intersect with Kodály chimes from the town hall clock. The *puszta*, even this early in April, is beginning to warm up – crossing their path, a young woman in a halter top inclines her sunglasses in their direction. Purity on the one side, flesh on the other – two competing strategies in the face of the sun.

*

In the city of goats, it's as if the ghosts of the original herd still nibble at the shrubs. One could imagine them advancing through the square, pleased to observe how the naked apes have built on their legacy. Their capering shadows mingle with those of the branches they munch at – the city becomes an assemblage of tents that can be taken down and hidden, once more, beyond the Carpathians.

*

Twenty-eight kilometres further south, the sun in Kiskunfélegyháza is already fierce enough, at eleven AM in early April, to scorch my face. So I take refuge in a *cukrászda* where a shy girl serves me coffee and lukewarm mineral water – I accept the water without complaint, needing to regain moisture as quickly as possible. I've spent an hour here already, in a place in which there is little to do – it seems – but go to work, go home and venture out again in the evening for an ice-cream or a beer. And the storks that I'd hoped to see here in spring are absent from rooftops, at least this close to the centre.

*

There's an hour-and-a-half to go before the bus back to Budapest. Eschewing the attractions of the local museum (with its farming implements and prison display) I walk the simple street-plan, throwing a mushroom pastry (disappointingly garnished with slivers of ham) into a waste-paper basket as a child, his ice-cream discarded by his mother, throws a colossal thunderstorm of a tantrum. I'm collecting another name, another place, another displacement.

*

In the Lira Bookshop, I search for a street map of Kiskunfélegyháza – not because I intend to return, but as a souvenir. A conversation in pidgin-Magyar reveals that there are none – instead, with a shrug, I'm shown a random collection of maps of other small provincial towns. No doubt, in one of those towns there is an unsaleable map of Kiskunfélegyháza.

*

The bus stops long enough for a shot of the *puszta*. It's like pointing a camera at the sea – endless grass and earth, a windbreak now and then, a whitewashed cottage set in its own miniature *puszta*. It recedes as if in time not space, back to the original hordes. No bell-tower in the distance, no madman tolling – only the overarching sky withholding, for now, its consolation prize of stars.

*

Half-asleep at dawn, I hear the soughing of traffic in Budapest's wet streets. Here, the noise sends me to sleep once more; at home, it would keep me awake. It is as if the noise, as well as the speech, is in another language.

*

Angular shadows on the Chain Bridge are as needles, pointing to tourists who photograph each other, convey their languages across the bridge and move on. Their shadows will be smoothed away by the footsteps of their successors.

*

The tourist is an idealist, who cannot imagine that the place they are in will exist when they have gone. The traveller is a realist, who knows that the place will outlast them.

*

A farcical encounter with the world's worst con-men – one of them an imitation money-changer, the other an imitation cop – enlivens an otherwise sterile walk across the Belváros. Both are so hapless, nervous and badly dressed that I swear in benign exasperation and walk off – they are far too sheepish to follow me. I end up almost feeling sorry for them – they are clearly time-travellers, looking for money to take back from my time into theirs and thereby grow rich.

*

A walk can arrange a city into myriad patterns. A predictable set of decisions, therefore, creates a predictable city. Today, the limited time at my disposal has led me to lose the city for a simulacrum. Coffee and cake, as so often, redeems the debacle.

*

Heavy rain, yesterday evening, washed away the shadows. Can rain ever be described as 'dark'? This rain felt dark, especially after a sunny morning spent in a gentler place – it weighed down everything and darkened hurrying faces. For an evening, autumn returned and today is cooler, fresher and cleaner as a result. The contrasts between heat and cold, or light and dark, are much stronger here than in England – and this applies, no less, in the equable month of April.

*

Attila József's statue remains, for now, outside the Parliament building. The government would like to remove it to a less prominent place, returning the square to how it was in the dictator Horthy's reign. I squeeze his bronze hand in solidarity. Moving him means tampering with the Danube itself.

*

In an underpass outside Nyugati station, a dozen Roma down-and-outs are singing, or perhaps howling, to keep up their spirits. Their howling dirge approximates the wind that enters the underpass from the north, chilling all to the bone. It is both plaintive and terrifying, a lament from a lower circle of Hell. No words can do justice to this desperate song – it is the song of those who have been exiled from the garden for good.

*

Every *dérive* is incomplete – a trampling of shadows by a shadow. All possible *dérives* amount, in total, to an authentic, complete and unknowable city – singly, these walks are like the encounters of a butterfly with a street-map spread out on the grass of a park that its pattern-work contains.

*

On the final morning, my camera jams – as if unable to cope with any more images. All should be preserved on the memory card, but it still unsettles me – I find myself on the Várhegy, suddenly reliant on my natural vision alone. This is a challenge in the twenty-first century, the age of the infinite image-bank.

*

When I set out this morning, I wondered how I would fill these seven hours, but by the logic of Metropolitan time one tram ride or Metro ride leads to another, one coffee to another, one vista to another, one interesting stranger glimpsed in the street to another and so, whole days can pass in a kind of feverish presence. Already, in the Korona Kávéház – with the tour groups having not yet materialised and the reassurance of cherry strudel on my fork – I can feel the plane taking off.

*

And so to the airport… where I consider this heap of images and words that I've accumulated. Running out of energy to write this journal, of any further desire to leave these shadows on the page, I settle for the anomie of the departure lounge – the ultimate Interzone. In this space, if I look for shadows I see only reflections.

A life within a life

A RECONSTRUCTION

Closing my eyes whilst leaving them open, I face the white page and conjure that morning into view. Once more, I'm catching the bus to the Buda Hills, having been exiled at the crack of dawn so that my partner can give an English lesson to a bleary-eyed Magyar. This is an opportunity not a hassle, I convince myself – the morning is dry and bright, although it is now September and the air temperature, despite the warmth of the sunlight, is probably in single figures. That doesn't stop me venturing out for the day in shirtsleeves and by the time it gets to eight o'clock I'm off the 21 bus at Normafa and through the glade to the strudel stall. The stall is closed at this hour and there are very few people about – half-a-dozen joggers, a couple of old men, no families with children – to the north, the TV tower on Hármashatár-hegy is sharply defined against the azure vault and, to the east, the city's buildings are a scattered white dust that pollution only partially blurs. I sit on a bench beside the communist-era relief map of the hills – a cast-iron curiosity with János-hegy, the highest point, like the fierce brown breast of an Amazon – light shines through beech and oak and I sit, still tired from an abbreviated sleep and in need of more coffee where none can be found. I am, once more, alone in a forest in Central Europe and, after catching my breath, I decide that the only way to avoid sinking into torpor is to take a walk. So I walk a mile or so to the north and back again, through woodland and glades on a colour-coded path, photographing the graffiti scratched on bark by lovers and friends from five and fifty years ago as joggers pass me, trailing breath from their lungs in the still-cool air. In all, this visit takes an hour and, at the end, the 21 bus is waiting for the descent, past the elite residences, bungalows and genteel apartment blocks, to Moskva tér. All this happens in ghost-form as I stare into the whiteness – my closed eyes open, my open eyes opened on two places at once, my mind in the shape of words.

COMRADE RAIN

Dunaújváros, April 2013

The rain's much worse than I'd expected. Within a minute of disembarking from the bus, I'm soaked. It's five degrees at noon, and I resolve to take as many photographs as I can before succumbing to hypothermia.

The Socreal architecture of this Stalinist New Town – 'born' in 1951, as Sztálinváros, to serve a steelworks itself the size of a town – reveals its faded crud-coloured stucco. Above all, the balconies stand out – as if each citizen had been a mini-Stalin, declaiming dialectically materialist truths to their neighbours. The balconies, after all, are too small to sit on comfortably.

The main streets are characterised by colonnades that cover the entrances to a couple of shops at the most – so, seeking shelter, I'm continually driven out into the rain. Exposed as equally in sunshine, this is a place that scorns the limitations of weather – there was no weather, after all, on the drawing-board of the proletariat.

My unopened notebook becomes a soggy dough as I wander, a bedraggled detective in a dissident's poem. 'To the Danube!' I command myself and, on a path without shelter, I stagger between rusted statues. If I were to encounter a pack of dogs I would get down on all fours and bark them into retreat, the betrayer of everything.

As I retreat – a rain-skinned body in search of warmth – I pass an assemblage of sculpted rustics with primitive tools. And rain, at least, replenishes the Danube.

Comrade Rain, in Stakhanovite mood, reminds me of the terror of absolutes – as much as the heroic murals and the four-square megalomania of this uncompromising, yet amenable town. *I will toast him once I'm safe from him*, I decide.

IN ÓBUDA'S BRICOLAGE

Again in Óbuda's bricolage, I try to equate the fragments of the Roman town of Aquincum – easternmost outpost of the Empire against the steppe tribes – with the Baroque square at its centre and, overwhelmingly, the Sixties high-rises that, in an architect's vision from the Kádár era, were going to stretch in a long line fifteen miles upriver to Szentendre replete with a little ABC and a hairdressers and an espresso bar in each eleven-storied human filing cabinet. And, despite the verve of that planner's vision – bringing together the present and the distant past – what I see now is chaotic, the arm of a statue in a glass case in a subway, another containing a fragment of a limestone tablet inscribed with scratchy Latin, and the jarring of the present with the past is so abrupt as to take me out of time altogether. So I wander, clicking my camera as if at random, worn rapidly away by the afternoon sun and wondering whether I am, in fact, in the third-century Roman settlement envisioning an insane, demonic future in which barbarians build tall towers and metallic monsters surge past in all directions. And, eventually, I collapse on a plastic seat in a subway, avoiding the gaze of the wino whose bonhomie might be inflicted in a matter of seconds – worn out by these tectonics, by the weirdness of these architectural languages that are scrunched together on this archaic set. Only a genius or a fool could decipher them, and today I assume that I am neither.

THE RED STEERING WHEEL

As times remain tough, the underpass at Örs vezér tere becomes more crowded and the desperate spread out their cloths. On some, there is produce – silently, I've laughed at the sight of two young policemen poring over a pile of corn-on-the-cobs that had clearly been abandoned, as if stunned by their torpedo shapes. On most, there's the bric-a-brac of households – books, magazines, children's toys, ornaments, dolls and worn-out clocks. Looking more closely, I see the same faces from day to day. I either walk through, heading for the bus or the suburban train, or turn into the mall whose micro-world is devoid of desperation.

I seldom witness a sale. Sometimes a commuter spends a few seconds looking, absentmindedly, at an object. In the ceaseless flow of faces, there are some that glance briefly at (for example) the old copies of *Playboy* or a soap dispenser but most have business to attend to. It's a zone where infinite patience leads to minimal profit – as the 'hardworking families' that politicians court spend their wages in the mall, or appear in rapture on propaganda posters as if they were the only Hungarians who had ever existed.

On one of the cloths this week, there's a bright red steering wheel. It's hard to tell what it fitted. Moreover, it's impossible to imagine it being bought but the vendor has brought it here and taken it back, when the crowds have thinned, on several occasions to who knows where. I toy with the idea of buying it, of bargaining in broken Magyar before I settle for the vendor's original price. I wonder if I would be committing a criminal offence in a country that, in theory at least, has criminalised the homeless. But I do nothing – just notice it again from day to day and, for the final time, *en route* to the airport. A red flag abandoned on stony ground, it is probably still there now.

ALMOST OUT OF BREATH

Munkács to Auschwitz, 1944

At the journey's end, there is just enough time for a photograph. These elderly men are standing, lying or sitting on a grass bank beside the shower-rooms and – as the caption makes abundantly clear – they have not convinced the doctor in the two or three seconds at their disposal. One line leads to the work-camp and the other leads here, to this grass bank where a ghoul with a camera snaps them for the murderers' posterity.

So they lurk in faded formal attire with turn-of-the-century beards, five minutes from eternity or oblivion, quietly alone with their thoughts, not necessary grasping their fates but utterly abandoned, nonetheless, and with their biographies about to fade… decades of memories, passions, certainties all reduced to these few minutes of utter powerlessness that is also a kind of triumph.

Not that they will have perceived it as such. Exhausted after their long excursion in a train with locked doors and no windows, they have been robbed of the last of their days and only these few seconds are left. It is not the final sip of a delicious drink that is savoured – they can only spend these moments in exhaustion and bewilderment, divested of lives that were rich with incident but defenceless against this administered obsolescence. Their names have already died and, whilst they survive for now, it is only as shapes that are minutes away from becoming smoke.

And yet, despite his infernal agenda, the photographer has conveyed them through seven decades to stand before us – armed with nothing but humanity's impermanence. And although we can't bring them back to life with our gaze, any more than the existence of this photograph can do so, we can spit in the face of death by way of our words, our thoughts, our flawed memorials.

A HERON'S ADVENTURE

There can surely be no connection between the sight of two great white egrets, taking off from the reed-bed at Dinnyés at the sound of the train on which I travelled back to the capital from a day-trip to Székesfehérvár, and the five-forint coin I'd discovered in my wallet on returning from my previous visit to Hungary.

It was the first time I'd seen great white egrets – streamlined, sharp-white creatures at least as large as the grey herons I'm used to and much larger than the egrets of Devon estuaries – and they were gone as soon as I noticed them, rising with dagger beaks under their umbrella wings. They flapped away to the south and the bright red train sped east, past Lake Velence to the suburbs of Budapest.

The five-forint coin has a great white egret on its face – which, at the time, I assume to be a heron. With four hundred forint to the English pound, it's the lowest denomination and I've no idea why it features a great white egret – storks, after all, are more typically Hungarian, building their nests in the farms and villages of the *puszta*. But I look upon that humble coin with irrational sympathy, perhaps in anticipation of a life to come or in memory of one that's passed.

Indeed, I decided to return this one to its homeland, handing it over to a down-and-out in the underpass near my partner's home. This, in itself, was a political gesture in the current context – but it was also a liberation. Was it, then, my reward to see these egrets in flight – but which one, I also wonder, was mine and which one yours, O fellow-sentimentalist with a five-forint coin in his wallet at the airport? Unless, that is, I find another coin on my return to England, one for which I have already been paid in advance.

AN INCREMENTAL VOYAGE

Over repeated visits, the novelty subsides and one accumulates incidental, incremental details in place of grand gestalts.

So what did I bring back this time? I list the following.... the newly-opened fourth Metro and a selection of its Gigeresque stations. The taste of pomegranate *kefir*, of piquant peppers stuffed with cream cheese from Szentes and smoked Gomolya cheese from the Hortobágy. The paintings of the Surnaturalists, depicting the Budapest of the early Sixties in intense neon colours. The interior of the Orthodox Synagogue in Erzsébetváros, a place that brought me close to tears to think that some Hungarians still resent the presence of Jews in their midst. The taste of a delicious strawberry pancake in the Árkád shopping mall, rain dripping down from stalls at Örs vezér tere and my partner's cats chasing each other around and knocking down plants. These, I admit, are all small details – but life's composed of such details and perhaps, I conclude, it's as easy to encounter the unfamiliar in the familiar, by way of minor variations such as these, as it is to take it in when one is stunned by the unfamiliar.

Each time could be the last and, if this is to be the last, my final sight of downtown Budapest will have been the interior of the Allee mall, the coffee I drank and the cheesecake I ate, the brief walk through the rain to the tram-stop, the ten-minute trip on an ancient model brought back into service with the windows half-blurred and the Danube misted up, the Museum of Arts and Crafts with its luridly-tiled Secession roof, the steps of the metro station at Corvin-negyed and the platform where, just one minute later, a steel-blue train pulled in. Details in layers… of a life within a life.

CODA

Ten minutes after our final parting, I sit and mark time with an ice tea – too burdened down with bags to contemplate further exploration. I'll proceed to another mall instead, appropriately named Terminal, and thence to the airport.

Another scribble on the map of Hungary, and on the map of Budapest in particular, will have been inscribed. And the sights and sounds that are so close to me now – the customers in this mall, the semi-familiar shop-signs – will be buried too deep in memory for exact retrieval.

On returning, I will move from a territory in which the words, still largely unfamiliar, are as objects in the world outside – opaque and ideogrammatic – to one in which they will simultaneously exist in the outside world and in my head. Despite the heat, the crowds and practical challenges, this place permits me to keep language at bay, in order to maintain a space around myself within which, as if somehow cleansed, I can imagine myself to be at peace.

The noise of my return will come soon enough, I think, and I drain my ice tea as slowly as possible. You are already about your business, preparing to share the language I will return to with those for whom it is unfamiliar. You know this place well enough, by now, to hear both languages and I wonder at how they must mingle in your mind.

You are only a couple of kilometres away from me at the most, on a metro train heading into the centre or perhaps, by now, on a tram or trolleybus. And yet, from the moment we parted, it was the same thousand miles that I've long since come to know, and, at the same time, not even the distance of a hair's breadth.

OLD STONES, WHITE ROADS

Kraków, March 2013

On the train from the airport, snow dribbled down the window and the suburbs, as if engrossed in chaos, welcomed me with a yawn of ice and graffiti. The station was depopulated, as if constructed for my entrance alone.

Then I sat at the window of a suburban hotel, wondering why it was that, at the end of March, I had been unlucky enough to encounter this whiteness. I had convinced myself, when booking the flight, that I would relax under a café umbrella in early spring sunshine.

Instead, the blue tram approaches the centre and I disembark, head bowed against sleet with the Wawel to my left. And I traipse the Royal Route – almost deserted in the late afternoon of Easter Sunday – wiping slush from my glasses, trying to find words for the discoloured ochre shades of the buildings.

The city, at least, is hushed and serious. In the Rynek, sleet intensifies before turning to a freezing, flatulent rain. Old stones, white roads, a handful of tourists under bright umbrellas inspecting stalls… I circle the edge before turning back in search of somewhere warm, cheap and authentically Polish in which to eat.

The city's make-up has been washed away. Its reality is all that remains – buildings that seem as immutable as the stones of a tor. I can almost pretend that I am not a tourist, but a secular pilgrim to a place of epiphany.

KAZIMIERZ

Set apart from the rest of the city, this neighbourhood is one in which ghosts have left footprints. The former occupants are gone, whether driven out or murdered – but it is recovering meaning, acquiring a modified identity as a place in which a Jewish renaissance meets the bohemian Poland of the twenty-first century.

We dine on borscht and potato pancakes in the Arial restaurant, to a murmur of klezmer muzak. The whip-cracking masters have been warded off for good and, as they shrink into the chronicles, their forms acquire the ephemerality of cobwebs. *They lost*, we eulogise – their totalising madness a distant memory, our casual presence here a riposte to their megalomania.

But, for anyone who knows a little of the history of this place, the death it contains is indelible. And how can we ever know where our own death resides? Can any place, however redeemed, escape that undertow?

Georg Trakl died from an overdose, in a military hospital in this city, in November 1914. He was buried for a decade in the Rakowicki Cemetery – a tram ride to the north – before being re-interred near Innsbruck. If he had been told in 1913 that Kraków, the Galician capital and leading city of *Młoda Polska*, would be the place in which he would meet his end – how surprised would he have been?

I, too, could die here in an instant – here one moment, falling to the ground the next – and there would be worse places, and even worse nights, I morbidly conclude although the time is always too soon. And tonight, at least, I escape – if not from the outnumbering dead.

THE REST OF THE WORLD

Drowsy, in mid-evening, at the end of another unexceptional day, I tell myself without intending to do so –

BEFORE I DIE, I WILL VISIT THE REST OF THE WORLD.

And my imagination pokes at the earth and its fecundity of places for which one life (I silently wail) could never be enough.

And I move at ten thousand miles a second, without leaving my armchair. And I am a stranger everywhere. And I am somehow still at home.

And the heavens surmount me, impossible destinations in their trillions, wherever I roam without roaming.

And in confusion and vertigo I collect my thoughts and decide on a place, just one small place, that can stand in for the others and convince me, once again, that I am truly at home on earth.

Truly at home, that is, for the duration of my mortality.

And so it is that, later and more awake, as the moon begins to wane and spring night thickens, I sit, listening to familiar music

that transports me to a shady hillside, somewhere to the south, on an evening that is longer and warmer than this one

where the sky cools down at sunset, as birds fall silent and bats begin to flitter

and I laugh my Pan-like posthumous laugh as, once more,

THE REST OF THE WORLD SURROUNDS ME... TRULY MINE FOR THE REST OF MY LIFE, AND AS NEAR AND FAR AS MY SHADOW.

On a Dry Sea

*on the green road to the east:
June 2012*

*

Distance is never absolute, even when grassland stretches from sunrise to sunset and the sound of hooves pounding lulls breath into a trance.

Distance leads to the pastures over the hill, great inland seas where sturgeon lurk, gap-toothed mountains and the fertile plain beyond.

These horsemen gallop encased in armour, like enormous lethal insects in chitin. They feed and sleep in the saddle and comfort, to them, is a cool breeze after a hundred-mile ride in corrosive heat.

They are relentless and merciless, picturing tidy piles of skulls at the gates of cities whose inhabitants dared to resist – an algebra of lopped heads and tribute keeps them going through the emerald monotony.

Distance at their feet, distance in their eyes, distance overhead where Tengri writes his scriptures in cirrus.

On their maps, the pristine continent of Europe is a mere excrescence. They recognise no boundaries. Distance is only an inconvenient fact and the gates have always been open.

*

In 1242, they stormed their way to the Danube, leaving smashed churches and the bones of peasants in wells. Desolation claimed the Carpathian Basin – the Last Days were incarnate. Hordes of Gog and Magog spread west and, even though they were men as other men they could only be seen as devils.

Were they devils to themselves or the only real people, casting aside ghosts and slaves on their way to fresh pasture? The victors write the biology textbooks, although their saddles were the only textbooks they required.

A death called them back before they could annex the sub-continent – what true continent could have been invaded in this way? Europeans were relieved – the Antichrist had been repelled, for now, by an unseen Hand. In the blighted provinces, new churches were built but, at evening, their wardens would look away from the setting sun and listen, attentively, for the murmuring of steppe-grass in the east.

Devils without a chink in their armour, moving at a devil's pace, reaping men without thought or doubt. Without horizon, but with a cursory ethics.

*

Gazelles, white-tailed and black-tailed, under a vault the colour of speedwells.

Marmot, snuffling in their burrows, hiding from piercing sun and infernal cold.

Cranes, spreading the white fans of their wings on ragged green, whooping into skies that might almost be solid.

Sun and moon, taking turns to move from one side of nothing to the other. Moving over no road, no city, no human voice.

A few weeks' ride to the west, the battlements of Buda and the ovens of Pest. Arrow-thoughted, with eyes that brook no limitation, a young man washes his horse and remembers. Kind to his friends and faithful to his lord.

Mutton-fat picked clean by the vultures of his desire, the continent a stretched-out hand containing his lifeline.

*

Dog-faced Tartars on feather grass. Hearing the bells four thousand miles to the west, they slaver.

They are still out there, say the custodians of nightmare – successive waves of equestrian thugs, waiting to spill through cracks in the Carpathians, dismantling the very concept of 'Europe'.

At the centre of the land-mass, there are parched square miles of fescue where gazelles dart in myriad-tailed herds. Under porcelain skies and in biting frost, horsemen, cat-napping eternally in their saddles, are waiting to pounce.

Only the marmots are Taoists there, watching the hunger take flight – all else is on the move, to fertile peripheries where tribute amasses.

*

Circling slowly on the way into Ferihegy, the flight from Gatwick conveys its shadow over the quilted flatland. On all sides, there is fertility – carefully-tended woods break up the monotony, and there are villages of red-roofed houses side-on to muddy roads. The city's direction shifts with the aeroplane's flight – then we encounter the arrivals hall, the hoardings on the road to the city, the main square with its statue and department store, the banks of the blue-brown river.

Away from the city, to the east, there's a faint haze in the air – the heat-haze of the *puszta*, settled over the landscape on this August afternoon. Without a contour, it stretches east and, in its fecund interminability, four thousand miles of almost-equal flatness – broken only by the jagged wall of the Carpathians – extend to the waving grasses of the eastern Mongolian steppe, a landscape different from this one yet implicit in it.

Is it a green cord tethering two continents, or a striation across a single one? Hubris provides one answer, geography another. We tell ourselves that we are landing in the heart of Europe but, as we land, Eurasia extends its welcome mat beneath our feet. And the *puszta* is only the name it takes in these parts.

*

By the end of our lifetimes, will this continent of Europe be described as the second sub-continent of Eurasia in the textbooks (or whatever replaces textbooks)?

For, as the power and wealth shifts east, the arguments for privileging this peninsula are disappearing. The world will be the one that is seen from Dubai, Astana, Beijing, Jakarta or Delhi as much as from Paris or New York. With that changed perspective, the hordes that *swarmed out of Asia* will be the hordes that moved from one part of Eurasia to another – colonists, like the Europeans, scouring for resources like our common ancestors in the African deserts.

Then the last millennium or so will have been the Age of the European Sub-Continent – from Charlemagne to Churchill, from the Romanesque to Dada, from Giotto to Kiefer, from impenetrable forests to GM plantations – and it will be written up, another historical narrative with a rise, a climax and a fall. And the steppe-grass will keep growing and dying with the seasons.

*

At the Dzungarian Gate, there is a pass through mountains with a railway line, a concrete platform, a Chinese locomotive waiting to be uncoupled from its carriages. Only the north wind is at home here, whipping through the gap from Siberia – its griffins, located here in classical times, are invisible and their masses are locked into the *clean* blue sky.

The wind's effect on concrete and metal is impossible to decipher, so it seems as if everything is calm – it is the kind of wind that one associates with the sea, except that it is a wind that ice has honed. Moreover, this is as far from the sea as it is possible to travel on this planet of water. It is a wind that simplifies and fixes its prey to the spot. It is barely kept in check by the monitor through which the photograph appears.

At the Dzungarian Gate, griffins hide from the camera in the time-honoured manner of mythical beasts. Between Kazakhstan and Xinjiang, as bogies are changed, passengers drink green tea to scrape salt from their throats.

So far from the open shores, all moisture is provisional... including that which renders us human. Mummified whilst alive, the creatures of this place are severed from origin. They are closest of all on earth to the silence of the sky.

*

Taller than all grasses, eyes widened to the sky and flesh attuned to extremes of heat and cold… such is this existence devoid of shelter. It inhabits a felt tent that can be taken down, in hours, and moved away on horseback as if it had never been there.

No maps are possible under such circumstances. When settlements move, the landscapes themselves become illegible. When there is no variation for hundreds of miles, a map at any scale beyond the largest becomes a random assemblage of contours and splashes. The landscape is an abstract banner woven by blind hands at midnight.

I share that existence vicariously, charting the endless lands to the west in my mind and watching the city on the river banks with its multiple spoils. What affects me most from here are the frosts – the sound of my breath as it crystallises in the air and crashes tinkling to the ground at dawn, the sight of my urine as it freezes in flight and sings an ochre song of its own.

*

"Conquest is as much to do with dispelling the silence from our thoughts as with a luxury we have shunned since birth" said the khan, to his enemy's severed head.

His enemy smiled, too late to be saved by fealty. The smile of a severed head is like a stopped clock, telling the time from time to time and commenting ironically from a distance only the marmot could understand in its prickly-pear-shaped burrow.

Seeing what was to be done and doing it made the khan what he is today – monstrous and inimitable – on his death, he will be buried in a shrine beyond idolatry and the retinue that carried his corpse will be put to death to conceal the secret.

Pretentious apes, spread out from their original deserts to the cold high lands of the largest continent – seeding concubines and slaves, they repeat themselves in empire after empire and ride their horses over bones with a nonchalant grunt. The pattern repeats itself and is immune to sarcasm.

Then what if I were to stand in the midst of the steppe, in 1242, and sing of the return of the Goddess? Or climb into the kurgan mound beside the skeletons of the chieftain's horse and wife and the chariot from which the blood was wiped, pleading the cause of reason and compassion? But it has to be done, at least in fantasy, for despair to be kept at bay.

*

The scale of words against the scale of space… thinking them into the sedge, one becomes both more bashful and more defiant.

Words that are embellishments, faint traces at the edge of a vast and imbecilic silence… words like stars at the margins of blank space, ignored by marmot and falcon as they conduct their business, and by horsemen grimly chomping at strips of wind-dried meat as they settle into their saddles.

I juxtapose the dry green sea that stretches east for thousands of miles against these steles. I wonder what I am travelling towards by way of these words, what splendid evasions and what delusory appropriations… I imagine them stretched out at the feet of a khan, inscribed on the steppe with horse-bones, making him laugh for a moment or two before his servants kick them away and lead me to the slaughtering-ground.

*

And then, there's peace in the great skies of Tengri… a single eagle, released, flies far into the air and is lost. Tibetans say that there are vultures that do not land even in death, that continue to fly upwards as if too light for the earth's gravity… this eagle, on the other hand, is scaling the steps of his ardour with the crampons of his cries.

I juxtapose my crowded island with the space that reaches from Budapest to the eastern grasslands of Mongolia, I cringe at what distance has meant to me and how a hundred miles can exhaust. But I am made of where I am and this climate, this landscape and this temperament fits me…

citizen of the drizzly Atlantic, hunched beside my estuary, sniffing warm tea on a jetstream afternoon as water soaks my windowpane.

This is why I crave for space I would never truly wish to possess. Horrified by the meaty diet, by extremes of sun and cold, I would cower in the nearest *ger* and retreat to the blandishments of Google Street View.

And yet… when I look east, my atlas-devouring mind escapes to the stone-faced spaces of Eurasia, dreaming of the geopolitical heartland and the death of our illusory continent… that very continent to which my identity clings. And that eagle hovers, like a mote in my eye that I cannot cast out.

*

So, as I take off once more from Ferihegy, the emphatic mosaic of the *puszta* captivates. Asia is at the gates of Europe, Mongols trample down the sunflower fields, Turks advance from the south, Russians – both European and Asian – deploy their tanks and, likewise, the English stride through the streets of Calcutta in their suits, Portuguese construct their churches on the island of Macao, the French introduce the art of croissant-making to the imperial capital of Hanoi. There is no border, only the ideology of a border. There are only apes out of Africa, fanning out in every direction and acquiring slightly-altered skins and a Babel of languages.

A green-beige slick that can be seen from space, the belt of the grasslands dwarves us with its distances. We praise it by not daring to traverse its infinite acres like the barbarians we can no longer be. I pick up the image of this island and drop it into the immensity with my eyes – it loses itself in fescue. To the invaders, it is merely a source of tribute – too far away, and cold, and wet, and devoid of horses to be worth invading.

Fascinated by the silence of that expanse, by the miles on the map, I must admit my failure and turn, like Marco Polo, to a west that exists in neural space – on a singular planet that cannot be divided, no longer where I am and no longer where I am not. My vertigo is the ape of silence.

Desire and harm

FLESH HORIZON

Nights in the temple. I recall the taste of your sweat, the way your mouth plunged into mine again and again. I was a lover but also an explorer and a scientist, discovering what the body could mean and that, just like the rest of us, I was immersed in a physical world whose dimensions preceded me. That to love and to die were clauses in the same sentence, a sentence conceptualised to the point of cliché. That it was enough to enjoy what the physical world had to offer, to pray to tangible gods and hold the charm in one's hands, turning it over and over until it spoke at the back of one's mind. That it was enough to construct a soundtrack to the vicissitudes of mortality, and to leave it behind for others to dance to. No, this didn't all come to me at the time, in bed with you that night at the age of twenty, but the seeds were sown and I couldn't go back to the spectral lure of the anima. And once more I plunge into the sweat of the nights of the tropical forest, descending through life to a delicious vacuity of sleep accompanied by the liqueurs of my dazzling blood… recalling the taste of your sweat, the thickness of your tongue, the pointlessness of work, ambition, and even art when faced with the directness of such encounters, the conditions of life made bare in a woman's flesh on a night in a temple of sweat-stained sweet-smelling bedclothes.

You, I say to myself, can forget me if you want. For my part, my ecstasies are there to be made use of. The temple door is open, and death waits like a punter at a strip-club whose presence, with querulous grace, I accept.

BY BRAZILIAN WATERS

Is this the bank of an enormous river or the brink of an ocean? At moonrise, I cannot tell. In tropical night, the birds are silent and I walk, naked, through Demerara-coloured sand. The arrows don't hurt and the poisons are delicious to my skin. They marble in my veins, they cause me to float and, if I were to scratch my skin, the stars would fall to ground and explode, their fragments devoured by ants and termites as the moon continues to rise and the goddess, who would laugh to be named, appears at the far end of the beach. She has deep brown skin, more chocolate than mahogany, and her black hair's a nest of vulpine electricity. She crooks her finger and laughs. 'Come on' she seems to say, 'you're falling for that same old trick, for the lure of something that you've chased and chased and which can only ever be one step beyond where you arrive, exultant as if fulfilled'. And what is promised in this encounter, as in all the others, is not the threshold crossed but the threshold *attained* – a point at which, at last, it seems that life will assume an ecstatic physicality but it isn't so, I reach the threshold and then the dream evaporates to leave me washing out the coffee-cups with the scent of the loved one fading fast. But, like a fool, a holy fool, I keep on walking towards her. And the moon keeps rising as I walk. The water keeps flowing on this tropical night. And I step across my skeleton, exposed in the sand, as I stumble into my after-world.

SIGHTINGS OF THE MYSTERY WOMAN

Again and again I see her, this woman who – as far as I can recall – I've never met, who inhabits the same city as I do and who has crossed my path to the point where I keep noticing her, to the point where mere coincidence (surely) cannot begin to explain it. This time, she is with a friend in a city centre pub at five on a Saturday afternoon – at other times, we have sat opposite each other on the bus, bumped into each other in WHSmith, or occupied adjoining tables in coffee shops. Being blonde, she orders pale food and drink, in the form of chicken and white wine – this, too, is surely beyond coincidence – and chats to her friend with her back turned, as I pick at my veggie burger and try to ignore her. She is young – perhaps in her late twenties – and attractive in her way, but I'm sure that this isn't the reason why I keep noticing her. Rather, she possesses the capacity to connect my present to my past, appearing in order to remind me where I was – however mundane the locations – at the time of my previous sightings. In this way, she is the guardian of my city, the one who expresses it to me as no-one else can, as no-one who knew me and was disturbed or distracted by my presence ever could. In her total indifference, she offers the resonance of pure encounter, the possibility of an Other that will never disappoint by manifesting. Perhaps she knows this without knowing this, I speculate, leaving her to her wine and conversation – on my way past her, I can't help but turn for an instant to look at her and it is as if I see myself in the pupil of her left eye, only with my back turned, travelling inwards, down a moving staircase I feel for a microsecond under my feet. Desire would be sacrilege and, in any case, beside the point. I head for the door and speculate as to the place of the next encounter, without the slightest doubt that there will be one.

LIGHTNESS OF TOUCH

Miles Davis on headphones, Friday night. His 'Great Expectations', leading me towards the rest of my life.

How many days, months, years, breaths, sighs, pauses, silences? How many advances and retreats? How many more loves and hates? I ask the white page. It blackens with my thoughts.

I consent, once more, to the pact of living. I feel lust although it is unfocused. The Moon and Venus are crossing my natal Venus – this suggests the invention of imaginary women who appear as twins at the back of my retina.

I am keen to remain faithful but I am also on alert for new loves, for the smell of their hair and the lustre of their skins. Everything remains unfocused, as in a dream. I am even uncertain of my sex, which has spread across my skin and is neither a lighthouse of isolation nor a volcano of honey.

I am marinated with their taste as the music swallows me – the rise and fall of Miles' trumpet, reaching a crescendo and falling back into the polyrhythmic murk. Mistress Luna, madam Aphrodite, re-assuring me that I am not too old to be enraptured. At least not yet.

OUT OF FOCUS

You meet a woman who tells you that you're beautiful, that you deserve to belong to the chosen. You're low on confidence and wondering where the next blast of inspiration will come from – moreover, it's winter and you can't shake off the sense that your feet have aligned themselves to a different geological period. She is the solution. She will complete you or negate you – you know that you will die and that this is the best way to control the experience. So she takes you back to her scruffy bed-sit and, with sufficient incense, you can imagine yourself in the Taj Mahal, the tent of an Arab princess or a well-upholstered New Orleans whorehouse. You fail to notice the monkey on the shelf as it points and sniggers, or the crow that pecks at the window. You fail to notice the scythe that winnows potted plants invisibly from the distance of Saturn. You are *in there*, drifting as if in and out of consciousness. She keeps telling you that you're the one, the zero, the other half, the solution to the equation, the dream that completes her dream.

So, before you can say *I cease to resist* you are led to the buggy, taken out to the desert and the ranch with no clean water supply, to be stripped of your name and your wallet and your history and your *polis* and, one evening, on a whim from her guru, you are buried up to your neck in a dune and left there as a gift of meat to his familiars. Only now do you notice that you need new spectacles and that you cannot tell the difference between a lover and a succubus or, for that matter, between a vulture, a kite and an angel of death.

A HECKLER IN EL CLUB SILENCIO

Mulholland Drive

Another singer collapses as the music plays on. That is how it is in El Club Silencio, in a night much deeper than night.

The audience, too stunned to applaud, is engulfed in its nocturne. And applause would only suggest a day to come that is at odds with the crimson drapes, the shabby balconies, the aura of a realm that is as self-contained as a satellite.

They share a single sleep in which torch songs circle like crows, deathlier than death because it is repetitive and blank (unlike death which, in comparison, is industrious, brisk and stupid). The songs that echo through this sleep are more powerful than the singers – who are carried out, in turn, and returned to the mannequin cupboards from whence they came.

The space behind the stage where the props are stacked is invisible, as are the dressing rooms where the dead prepare to reiterate their deaths. It is all too tempting to shout for the orchestra that *has to* exist, that will play the orchestra's notes as the audience shivers.

Thought spins to the heart of the theatre of sleep. Outside, it is always three AM and frost insinuates itself between the naked toes of a tramp. Buildings mass like trees in a forest – the sun's a scarab under a stone.

In any dream, it is possible to shout oneself awake and, by supreme bloody-mindedness, the diurnal voice is raised. As cobwebs colonise the air, the curtain melts in a nimbus of dust. The audience jolts awake, separate both in body and mind. And even if the songs continue to play, there is no-one sufficiently asleep to hear them.

THE GATECRASHERS

Once again, in the overgrowth beside the ruined barn, I stand at sunset – as still as the thistles on the tangled path I clambered through to be here – and observe the wildlife. There isn't that much – a few moths, a wren behind a bush, a pipistrelle that darts across my vision before plunging for food – but they remind me that my species is not the only one on the planet. 'At least not yet', I think, as I consider the sixth mass extinction and the prospect that we will cover the earth with our shadows – shadows under which no other life will prosper.

And I think of the exhausted creatures. The butchered creatures. The appropriated creatures. The creatures re-shaped for our benefit. The creatures made of meat. The creatures made for experiment. The creatures that are pets, and the creatures that are pests and therefore deserve to be hated and to die… as the child in the shopping precinct, bullying the hungry pigeon that crosses its path, can attest with its parents' indulgence.

And, standing in a small-scale wilderness, I think of the wildernesses hacked to death and the creatures caught beneath the wheels of our tractors. I think of the creatures trussed and flayed in Cantonese markets. I think of all the 'philosophical' reasons put forward as to why we are superior to other creatures, and special, and unique, and made in the image of God.

And, having nothing else to apologise to, but happy to apologise to the lightest of all mammals, I look up at the pipistrelle as it passes overhead and try to imagine what it makes of me. A great fat ape in the undergrowth is what it would observe – if not for my clothes, remarkably like the first one who passed here several thousand years ago and looked up, in an empty land, at the sunset's emissaries.

THREE DENOUEMENTS (after Herzog)

I'm on the raft, the water is rising and packs of green monkeys are skittering everywhere. My men are either dead or exhausted. My beloved lies, wounded, with glassy eyes and an arrow I don't dare to pluck out. I tell the river that I will escape from this impasse, sail to the far-off kingdom and claim the throne which has always been mine to lose. 'Who is with me?' I ask, knowing that my men are lost and that the monkeys serve their own curiosity and hunger. I can barely take refuge in a fantasy of renewal and triumph, a history that's staged as lesser men stage plays.

Then I'm on the operating table, prone and sodden with invisible water, listening with my feet to the sound of the surgeons explaining me away by the shape of my brain, the imbalance of hemispheres. One takes my brain aside and cuts it up like a cauliflower, isolating elements that came together to make me strange – or attempting to do so. The scribe is so excited at the diagnosis that he decides to walk home just this once, drooling over the beautiful, precise protocol that he will write to define my meaning once and for all.

It's as well, then, that I come to in a merchant's house with furniture one would shudder to sit on in case it cracked. Is it in Wislar, Delft, or Weimar Berlin? Who knows. The important thing is that the rats are still at large and that I am somehow conversant with their language. I open my mouth and smile with a mouth of teeth that could never belong to a passive skull. There's work to be done and, once more, I'm on the dry land of my own ambition.

KASPAR AND THE VOLUMES

My latest book is covered, in moments, by another book. And then another book covers that book which, in turn, is covered by another book. Then a magazine leaps on that book like an owl on a mouse. Then a book leaps on top of that magazine like a falcon on a vole. Then an even bigger book, a book that looks as if it might take a lifetime to read, leaps on the other book like a rugby player scoring a try. Books rain down on every side as my latest book is forgotten, crushed, unread and slighted even by myself who would have forgotten I'd even written it if I hadn't been reminded by the sight of all those other books that leapt on top of it without mercy.

That's how it is when there are hundreds of thousands, millions even, of talented people on the same planet all clamouring for attention. I'm amused, not angry, so amused that I fail to notice that I'm losing the power of speech and can no longer even contemplate the manipulation of a keyboard. Eventually, a pen – even a well-made, smoothly-flowing gel-pen – is too much to handle and I let it drop into the (figurative) straw where, surrounded by books and the ghosts of books and the promises of books weighed down by books and the threats that will turn into books and the worms that will turn into books and the books that will turn into worms, I grunt incoherently and drive my companion back and forth across the straw, no longer able to contemplate why I got here in the first place, and why my feet are so chafed, and why there is a chain attached to my braces that I cannot reach to unfasten.

Here, I only have memories of one other – his black cape smothers me sometimes. He strikes my hand with his cane. He guides my hand as he teaches me the word that all the words, in all the other books, amount to. 'Schreiben' he tells me, 'Schrei-ben'. 'ROSS!' I reply, countering with a word that no book can encompass, as volumes decompose in the earth-sized space around me.

BARILOCHE

This doesn't have to be a true story. The redundant dictator is in exile, in a villa on the shores of a deep blue lake surrounded by snow-capped mountains. He is many hours' drive from the capital and many hours' flight from the principal scenes of his biography. And to all intents and purposes his biography is over. His dreams of returning to power have gone. His material needs are satisfied but he is tired, and ill, and far too old to do anything apart from wait for death. But death refuses to come. He eats his solitary meals surrounded by guards and dreams of the destiny he had or thought he had – once the most powerful of men, now no more than a malevolent ghost. Having long since been declared dead, he could no more reappear as his former self than any corpse and what would await him, in any case, would be an even more humiliating end. So he waits here to die, having denied so many others the choice of waiting to die through his persuasive madness – no longer rehearsing speeches but the silence and oblivion that will attend him soon. This is a crueller and a more deserving fate than the trials of his lieutenants at Nuremberg.

TANGERINE DREAM IN THE THIRD REICH

As the Normandy beaches filled with landing craft, another warrior of the Reich was born in the Prussian town of Tilsit. And, despite all predictions to the contrary, the invasion was repelled. Despite the foes that were ranged against it, the Reich prevailed. A thousand-year order was established as the Führer had planned.

Into its silver age, harnessing electronic equipment prepared with sonic attack in mind, the ensemble Tangerine Dream came into being. They claimed that they were named from a line in a long-lost Gothic chronicle, describing the truest shade of the summer dawn. The child of the town of Tilsit, Edgar Froese, led them into musical battle against the recycled forces of the nineteenth century. And, remarkably, prevailed. Their greatest triumph was in 1974, when they played their composition *Phaedra* at the Führer's eighty-fifth birthday concert. And even that lowbrow chicken breeder Himmler applauded, relishing the link between the Fatherland and Classical Greece.

In this parallel world, we cannot imagine what that music would have sounded like. We can only hear music made by another Edgar Froese, another Chris Franke and another Peter Baumann. Music born on the very day that the Europe that made this music possible came into being. Music that seems inconceivable in the absence of freedom.

Edgar Froese, the driving force behind Tangerine Dream, was born in Tilsit, East Prussia on D-Day – 6th June 1944.

A Citizen's Diary

*Plymouth, Summer 2013:
revised 2015 and 2017*

*

It's been a week spent on familiar circuits, from workplace to home to shop to *polis*. As I sit on the bus I contemplate the street map's contortions, the sclerosis of a city whose centre, as with most other port cities, is at its edge. Starting over, there would not be a city of this size in this location, as there would be neither the need nor the justification for it – but it wants to go on living, out of sight of power and influence but still the home of a quarter of a million people. What can it do to make itself useful? By simply being here, I am implicated in that challenge.

*

I try to think in terms of Plymouth, of the story of Plymouth, of the risks and opportunities of Plymouth, of the *character* and the *atmosphere* of Plymouth. Perhaps it makes most sense when seen from the heights of Mount Edgcumbe – stretching from one estuary to another, facing the ocean – a singular entity, like the labyrinth depicted on the street-map I project on the wall in front of me. And were it to disappear altogether, I think, I would be able to survey it as a single phenomenon and determine, finally, what it meant to me as my own life intersected with it.

*

So I contemplate the street-map in its confusion – the centre at the edge, a nondescript flyover at its natural centre, estates that sprawl into fields and hills. I can trace its patterns with my eyes closed, envisaging countless journeys from one suburb to another. That experience means more to me than the 'identity' of this place – the civic myths, the alibis with which it tranquillises itself.

*

Light burns on the *corniche* of Madeira Road. At Fisherman's Wharf, tombstoners impress an audience of potential ghouls. I know that it's mad to be out of the shade but still, I make it to the Hoe where the candy-striped lighthouse, relieved of its function, is the centre-piece of a human flourishing. I am at home and at the same time placeless – too spaced out by the heat to know exactly what 'home' might be.

*

Then I sit before the masts in Sutton Harbour, cradling my Asahi lager like a TV detective. Forty-five years ago, my parents would drive down here on a Friday morning to purchase fish for the evening meal. It's not a gesture that I'll repeat, as a vegetarian of thirty years' standing, but it made use of the city – bringing out its pungency in the shapes and smells of creatures caught not far from its shores.

*

A sparrow hops upon my table at the Bagatelle and engages in a capricious dance, moving parallel to my plate. I enjoy this mercurial encounter – the shape of a bird whose heart beats many times faster than my own, who must see my world as I would see the world of a tortoise. Suddenly, it flies off to inspect a crumb in the gutter – I go on wondering what it makes of this street, whose dimensions are those of a vast space speckled with food.

*

Circling once more – New George Street to Market Avenue to Cornwall Street to the mall to Old Town Street and back again to the sundial – I look up at the fluted columns and the worn insignia. A child for whom this city was built, I am growing older with it and there is nothing, not even death, that can rewind our stories to the beginning.

*

At Bretonside Bus Station, piped music is played. Waiting for my bus to depart, I hear America's 'Horse With No Name' outside – 'the first thing I met was a fly with a buzz' as a trapped fly moves from window to window in silence. Forty years later, this song's still fresh. It is in this city that I heard it first, taking it into my consciousness and imagining its desert landscape – so that, even now, it is still a part of this city despite its exotic origin and subject matter. Then it dies in my ears like a dried-up stream.

*

I cannot explain my dreams of this place. I roam through a phantasmal landscape, constructed mainly in early childhood, which is a vast and distorted version of this city – it also contains spliced fragments of other landscapes, perhaps encountered on television or in films. These landscapes can be more memorable than what happens in them. They will die when I die, obliterated kingdoms that no séance could ever reveal.

*

Another nocturnal journey splinters as I wake. As I press the snooze button on my alarm clock for a third time, I lose sight of its architecture but can still place the site of its invention on a map. Again, I glimpse that city of which I am the only custodian and which intersects, uncannily, with the one I inhabit. As I walk to work, I follow the ships that sail from its shores with my eyes turned both outwards and inwards.

*

'Ocean city' – wanting to be made sense of, wanting to be of use, and wanting the expensive yachts that were built here to remain. Wanting all the roads that lead out of it to be like sea-lanes.

*

I struggle with the martial traditions – the military flags on the Hoe, the arrival and departure of warships, overpriced nuclear submarines in sheds and the gleam of buttons on jackets. I would love this city even more if it had been built exclusively on trade. Smyrna, Salonica, Cavafy's Alexandria or Bowles' Tangier – commerce and decadence, the aromatic sacks piled high, all comers welcome.

*

Cities layered on cities, in four dimensions, stretching back before my birth and the birth of my parents, before the coming of their forebears to the city from rural locations… it is as if these layers still exist and could be penetrated, as if I could look out one day from my place of work and see a smaller city amongst fields and hills. And there I would be in 1439, the city's history *before* me at last.

*

The sea, as ever, makes some sense of it. A ten-minute walk from the city centre reveals the start of ten thousand miles of water – a terrain into which a ferry or a frigate can emerge, growing from a speck of dust to an island in motion. It is as if this city came into existence as a bulwark against a void that would render its entrenchment and its 'warrior maid' pretensions meaningless. How pointless, then, to celebrate that entrenchment – as if it were possible to repel an invader without repelling a part of oneself, the dark dwarf in the distorted mirror.

*

From the charismatic waterfront, the city spills across its knolls and extends for six or seven miles in every direction. The Valium estates at its edge are compensated with immaculate views. They lead down to a narrow strip of grey at the southern horizon, an escape-route that's the colour of the bars of a cage.

*

Under a swoosh of horizons I recall the mutable face of the water, seen from boat trips on burning summer's days – on landing, I continued to walk on its undulating surface. And so it was that infinitude pursued me down the narrow streets of the Barbican, where I spilled from myself and became a rudderless craft. The feeling would be there at night, as I closed my eyes and sailed into night's anonymity.

*

Over the turquoise veldt of the Sound, I inscribe directions – to France or Morocco, New Zealand or Antarctica. Past the masts of the pleasure craft and the faint mark of the Eddystone Lighthouse, there is an infinitude of destinations and in each of them almost every trace of the city is erased. Mapping voyages through spray, I connect this port of origin with the wider world.

*

The shoreline, unravelled, might stretch for fifty miles like the shoreline of a metropolis. With a strip city behind it, a Muscat or a Genoa, answering only to the tides.

*

To live well in a city means to construct a ritual made from smaller rituals… inscribing one's habits and preferences on a map the size of a city. This traces an indelible, unique signature that connects a citizen to his or her locale… as long as it is never seen as an end in itself, as a means of defusing a life that is *always* too brief.

*

There are those who live here and are incapable of living happily anywhere else. There are those who live here but could live happily in another place, if not any place on the surface of the earth. And the rest, who are either passing through or long to escape. In their daily interactions, they are inseparable and – inscribing personal routes – create a city of movement and perspective.

*

At a roadside garage between Plymstock and Plympton, one afternoon in the early Sixties, a radio plays 'If Anyone Had A Heart' – the singer unknown to me then. I can't remember anything else from that day – where we'd been, what mood I was in, what my parents were saying. But perhaps I was taking possession of a delicate art – *the decision to create a memory* – for the very first time.

*

Giving me a lift home – and probably too tired to do so, but for how much longer will he take the wheel? – my eighty-five-year-old father takes a wrong turn. His working life, as an electrician, involved driving around the city from appliance to appliance – and the knowledge he acquired, over several decades, is that of a taxi-driver. Quickly, the map in his head lights up once more and he finds his way out.

*

A woman tosses her waist-length salmon-pink hair and, on shoulders and midriff, her tattoos appear abstract rather than the usual clichés (hearts, swallows etc). *Goth-graffiti skin in sunlight*, I think. We board the bus together and, making way for her, I catch her deeply-shadowed eye as she smiles back fleetingly. Her hair is of a completely different colour to the rest of the city. I cannot get her out of my mind and, at night, I fall asleep enveloped by waterfalls of salmon-pink hair, swimming upstream against her tidal beauty.

*

From an inlet where wine was imported for boozy priors, to a rampant warren of privateers and press-gangs, to a war-town replete with dockyards and ensigns, to an expanse of rubble and mass-graves, to a shining post-war vision of a city with immaculate boulevards, to recession cut with intermissions of plenty… the film moves on to a tomorrow I will never know. A twenty-first century baby is brought onto a bus and his mother – who is easily young enough to be my daughter – rocks his pram gently. 'It's all yours, son', I tell him under my breath like the citizen I am.

*

On the escalator of WHSmith, I see a trio of Mormon missionaries. 'They're on a stairway to heaven', I think, as they head to check out the map section. Five minutes later, in Waterstones, that's exactly the song being played in the Costa Coffee outlet – that song, out of many thousands possible. Out of small and random coincidences, we construct the cathedrals of memory.

*

Almost all of what has happened to me here could have happened in another city… a medium sized city, a European city, a port city, a working-class city, a remote city, a charismatic city. So *why not* here?

*

From the graveyard of St Budeaux church, Kit Hill is to the left and Dartmoor to the right. The Tamar and Tavy flow between them and the corral of Ernesettle – one of the post-war Abercrombie estates – is directly ahead. The material of the city is reconfigured, on the journey from lookout to lookout – perspectives multiply and, this afternoon, it is the most beautiful Panopticon that could ever exist.

*

Later, I'm beside the Plym at Laira – the tide out, the amphitheatre opposite. There are egrets, cormorants, an isolated heron. A single log in the mud – Plympton to the left with the redbrick chimney of my old school, Staddon Heights with its mast to the right. I stand on the embankment, sharing the time of estuarine birds… a time comprised of winged arrivals and departures and the suck of the moon on water. From here, as I write this down, I can abolish the traffic.

*

Back on the Hoe, near where the Beatles sat, I listen to a cover version of the Who's 'My Generation' played to an audience of bikers on a Thursday evening in August. Blanche and Jack, to whom this bench is dedicated, hope that I am enjoying the view. A luxury cruise-liner in the Sound is the size of Drake's Island. I try to imagine Blanche and Jack, the adults in life's prime that I might have encountered as a child or in a Sixties photograph. And, of course, I am enjoying the view.

*

In the summer of 1989 I tried to sum up the city in a single poem entitled, simply, 'Plymouth'. It seemed possible at that time, and from that distance – I had been living in the Midlands for over six years – and nor was the gesture false. But the effort seems ludicrous now, when the subject-matter of my carefully-structured poem surrounds me on every side and stretches for miles.

*

For the city is *everything* that can be said about it, a narrative that swirls in its streets and mutates over time into many millions of words. I have added my presence and my words, as I will add my absence and my silence too in time – bereft of neat solutions, enjoying my place in the labyrinth.

Renditions of home

CLIMBING THE SKY

Beyond the tree-line and the consolations of shelter, the brow becomes a mirror. Its sweat is a lake on which the brain-ship floats.

We walk with our backs to the sun, over tussocked ground, to the music of wings. Each step we take reduces us to the stripped-down countenance of shadow. In each black signature we cast, there's an infusion of metal retched up from chthonic seams.

The summit consists of a cairn and several puddles. To the north, the valley fans out and the spoil at Red Lake casts the faintest of shadows on parched ground. Two hours' walk is too far, we say with regret – and return to the stone row, each crooked peg of it a memorial for a melted heart.

We grow thinner and more exposed, mere twigs in motion.

Nothing dares to rescue us. Geology holds back. Birds part the air like a sea. We have inherited a kingdom in which, in turn, we will shimmer like ghosts. Whose turn will come first is of pressing importance, but only for a while.

UBIQUITY

On a mild November afternoon on the Cornish coast, in the tiny port of Charlestown, I locate myself in the digital photographs that are taken everywhere and in which I'm repeated, a random presence of tints and shadows, anonymous as leaves or a tide-mark on a beach. In those photographs – so often taken, like mine, in a moment of misplaced enthusiasm – I exist, unconsciously, in multitudes. I do so, of course, in photographs that seldom outlive their moment. Thousands are taken, almost all of them stored for a rainy day of recollection that will never come. How many of them would have existed in the not-so-distant past when there were twenty-five or forty exposures to a film? But, ignored on hard drives or on memory cards, they exist despite being overlooked and that is how I also exist within them. I sip my tea in shirtsleeves, on a mild November afternoon in the infinitely-replicable port of Charlestown, and consider my infinite replicability. It neither helps nor reassures but, nonetheless, I find it amusing that I am (at least potentially) ubiquitous.

COLLECTING THE PAST IN MY HANDS

Walking down Vinery Lane, between Plympton and Plymstock, on a sunny May afternoon I ask myself if I've ever been this way before and speculate that I have, in childhood. I hit upon the year 1970, perhaps because I have this unaccountable feeling from time to time that the last forty-five years have been a dream. But what would 1970 *feel* like, I wonder... craving the exact detail, from the clothes I'm wearing to designs on yoghurt cartons, from TV schedules (two channels in my household, both in black and white) to cars on the road to the chocolate machine I used to walk to on a Sunday evening to the orange football that I kicked around the tennis courts at Christmas. I look into my hands as if they were mirrors – falling through them, through the suddenly-imaginary years, to the source of my ten-year-old self as if there were all to play for and the futures that existed then (computers the size of spaceships, meals the size of pills and roll-neck sweaters and sideburns for everyone) remained plausible. If I think hard enough, perhaps, a chocolate wrapper will fall from the sky... or even an Aztec bar, still edible, from its portentous advert. Then I'll head home to *Catweazle*, and the satanic Cornish twins on *Crossroads*, and the skimpy shorts of the World Cup squad with the sound of their Back Home single in my ears. Whilst thinking of this, of course, I'm sure to dodge the illusory traffic of 2015 – or do I walk through it, at last immune from the present?

WHEN EVERY SONG WAS NEW

I'm lying in bed on a weekday morning, leafing through a bargain bundle of just-delivered football programmes and listening to Radio One. Yesterday, I feigned illness and it turned out, for once, that I was actually ill – so I'll be off for the rest of the week, concocting days of my own design. That's what happens when school's a bore and one has learnt how to cough.

The trials and tribulations of an assortment of football teams I do not support – Millwall, Charlton Athletic, Coventry City – engage me, briefly, as I flick through the pages. What absorbs me even more, in the thirteenth year of my life, is music on the radio – a radio I had just acquired. Radio One's eclectic mix of the time – from Isaac Hayes to Bowie, from Carole King to Procol Harum – teaches me, not to sing, but a multiplicity of worlds. Each track conveys me to a different place, more quickly than any television programme – to an ambience brought home to me in seconds by a snatch of melody, a line of lyric, a special effect from a Seventies studio.

Then I hear a single that only briefly enters the charts, that I might have heard just once at the time. 'Break', by Aphrodite's Child, fills my room with the warmth and colour of the Mediterranean and, as the sun ignites my window pane, I travel in thought to a south-facing coast that both is and is not my own. Borne there by its breathy vocals, I put my reading matter aside and imagine, for two minutes or so, what it would be like to flourish beneath a stronger sun, in an altogether clearer and more invigorating light.

How the world stretches past me at that point... receiving me yet drawing me out of myself into its infinite surprise. If I could have said so at the time, I would have said that this horizon can never, *must* never, be allowed to fade away.

A PROMENADE IN DUNSBURGH

Beating the bounds, we find the city to our left is suddenly a name without issue. Strawberry patches conceal it with damp green leaves.

To our right, the fields of the in-country stretch with immemorial identities. There's a twist and a tangle of lanes between them and buzzards that take no heed of human description.

It's a simple walk on a winter's afternoon – there's much to be said, but the words will be forgotten. Shadows made from the west creep up on us from behind – or flower like peacocks' tails, depending on mood and myth.

The wind is low. There's a vague chill in the air, enveloping the deeper mystery of what it means to live through a day on earth – an unrepeatable day, with the codes in our genes conspiring to brush us aside.

GIRDERS BETWEEN THE STARS

Under that lethal white construction I walked, as Dorset froze around me – the lights of Thornford and Yetminster like struck matches, stalks in fields as immense as stalagmites. It was an evening on which it seemed possible that the sun would never return… that on sinking below the horizon it had been eaten for good. We assume that it will come back, I thought, as we assume that the days will get longer once the Solstice has passed. But will it always be that way?

It was December 1982 and I was heading, of all the ridiculous things, to a party thrown by a woman I found attractive (and with whom all hope had already gone). As I walked at a steady pace, I moved more and more slowly inside. My nostrils ached, my hair was smooth to the touch, my hands were dispersed into the cosmos… fingering space between the stars in sinister, treacherous, indifferently homicidal Wessex. The earth was an extension of outer space – its absolute zero brought down into the nerves and blood-stream.

I can only pretend that I reached my destination and continued on the course that has brought me here. Somewhere out there, my skull is being kicked down the road like a crystal ball that failed in its prophecies. In a void between Yeovil and Maiden Newton, I know nothing of today. And tomorrow knows that I have never written this.

THE HIDDEN LAND HIDES ME

There is steady rain on a mountain path, between dark conifers.

Abandoned workings creak from the wind's weight. There's a clapperboard hut at the track's end, with a rust-roofed porch and a gnarled wooden door. Nothing can be heard but wind and birds, a rustle of insects gnawing under stones.

I hide in the hidden land. It could be the Sierra Nevada, or a fold in a map that's been opened by the rain, and the distance inside me that has drawn me here... suddenly here, as if in trance, on this stony path that leads away from the other seven billion. They, too, must surely long at times for hidden lands of their own. Or so I try to convince myself.

Inside this hut, exposed to a space that stretches overhead to the ever-receding ever-unknowable source, I dream myself back to namelessness and formlessness.

Around me are the ghosts of miners and chorus-girls still seeking their fortune. They attend me swift as bats, reminding me that we are destined, every one of us, to be forgotten no matter how splendid or how lasting our works. Because, even when remembered, we are remembered only as myth.

So I hide here in the hidden land, letting my name run from me like a wolf.

KEEPING VIGIL

I squander the afternoon with music, as horizontal rain assails the window and lights come on in the mall behind the ruined church.

I'm on strike this afternoon against the chimes of the clock. If I do nothing, I persuade myself, then time will come to a halt.

But everything still darkens. I listen to jazz through headphones, faint dregs cooling in the cup to my right, the football scores in flux until the inaudible full-time whistles.

I find myself in evening, looking out at the Plymouth skyline and the tiny lights on the Barbican. I think of the promenaders walking quickly to avoid the rain, and plastic chairs and tables unoccupied on the quayside.

Elsewhere, forensic chalk is drawn around atrocities. Bloodstains on floors of bars and concert halls are analysed. Stunned people gather on Parisian corners and in squares, on what was supposed to be their weekend.

When, if ever, will these homicidal myths give way? I have seen the day to its close and, drawing the curtains at last, abolish the world that fills me with renewed despair and desperate compassion.

At least the city I live is intact – its seagulls still on familiar flight-paths. I decide that I will draw back the curtains again at midnight, and that a brilliant Aegean sky is going to confront me.

OUT OF MY HANDS

A cold wet winter's night. A constant supply of tea. A decanter of laudanum, the colour of rubies. Someone's been here before, I think, as I count my fingers and reach for a metaphysical tome. But I bask in the magic of this solitude, imagine mountains mottled with sleet. And years to come with their inscrutable contours.

Reaching for the spectral decanter, I dislodge the book with its ponderous distinctions... and laudanum splashes on the carpet. 'There goes the deposit', I think... but it licks itself up like a komodo dragon and I'm left with the tea in my cup.

Savouring its amber abyss, I think of the atoll Pukapuka where there is only one walk to be walked, and where young men and women make love in twosomes, threesomes and foursomes for the sake of exercise. There's nothing untoward about those vague brown bodies... except that if I were there I'd be at least thirty years older, an old man in their eyes.

Where did my life go? How can I find it in that heavy book that melts into the carpet, or the ruined church that stands on a roundabout at the end of the street? Or the diaries, for that matter, heaped in my wardrobe? And the mountains – how long will they be there? I ask, for the thousandth time tonight.

Drunkenness is no excuse against the void – and neither is lust, no matter what the troubadours of Beulah might say. Time is outrunning me. The opiates have been drained from my cup and I stare into the looking-glass of my own extinction.

ALTOGETHER ELSEWHERE

My life's in one place, my mind in another. Once more, I face the music that pours in through headphones to remind me of a vast and golden land that I may never visit. For it becomes less safe to do so by the year. Those who would do me harm have appropriated almost every sand-grain… each burning rock, each lizard and gazelle, and its brilliantly streaming skies.

My life runs its course in a single region of the world. Yes, I could break out briefly with my two-weeks-at-a-time vacations, but what would that mean? Better to let the wider world flood into my mind, to be part of that world wherever I am. Even if this means that I am half-oblivious to my actual surroundings… and still more reluctant to devote the entirety of my writing to them.

To the south, the desert night displays its infinite plumage – a great wing of stars curves overhead and smothers the dunes. I imagine my enemies – although it is nothing personal – around a campfire, or turning their prayer-mats to the Source. An unbeliever insinuates himself amongst them as he sits in a room in a land of 'immorality and iniquity', wondering how the map of the world will look at the hour of his death.

So he reaches out for bread that is passed from hand to hand… but, of course, it eludes him. He watches tea poured into a glass, as if from a waterfall's height, from which he can only drink with his imagination. He measures the space and, as ever, the stars look down on believer and unbeliever alike… on those who thirst for paradise and those who go in fear of eternal sleep.

It is an average star in an average corner of the galaxy, he thinks, that roasts these warriors during the day and – perhaps – bestows on them their obsession with God. He contemplates his disappearance with a calm that suggests that he has already disappeared.

UNSEEN

This is the time of day when the places that I have not seen crowd into my mind. I will not attempt to describe them. They are different from one day to the next, because I will think of different places. They are different from the places that you will think of as you meditate, in your own time, on the gaps in your experience that will remain at the hour of your death. We all fall short, novices in the world who understand nothing. We skim the surface and the whole eludes us. We go to our deaths thinking that we have seen something of the world but, if we lived for a million years, that would not be true. But that's no reason to despair, I re-assure myself as I crack open a beer and decide to switch the computer off. Nothing was ever promised – what was expected was phantasmal and what was unexpected became inevitable too soon. I pull the curtains and the world disappears, although I know that it is there. At sunset in June, one bird sings to the next in turn and their songs reach out, in relay and migration, to the places that I have not seen and alert them to my presence. And I console myself that this will suffice, because nothing was ever promised and we can only ever make a start. I have made a start by constructing this text, a screen that they can lie behind and surprise me as I gaze from one side of the page to the other, from my shadow to yours.

Lightning Source UK Ltd.
Milton Keynes UK
UKHW011041111021
392014UK00001B/9